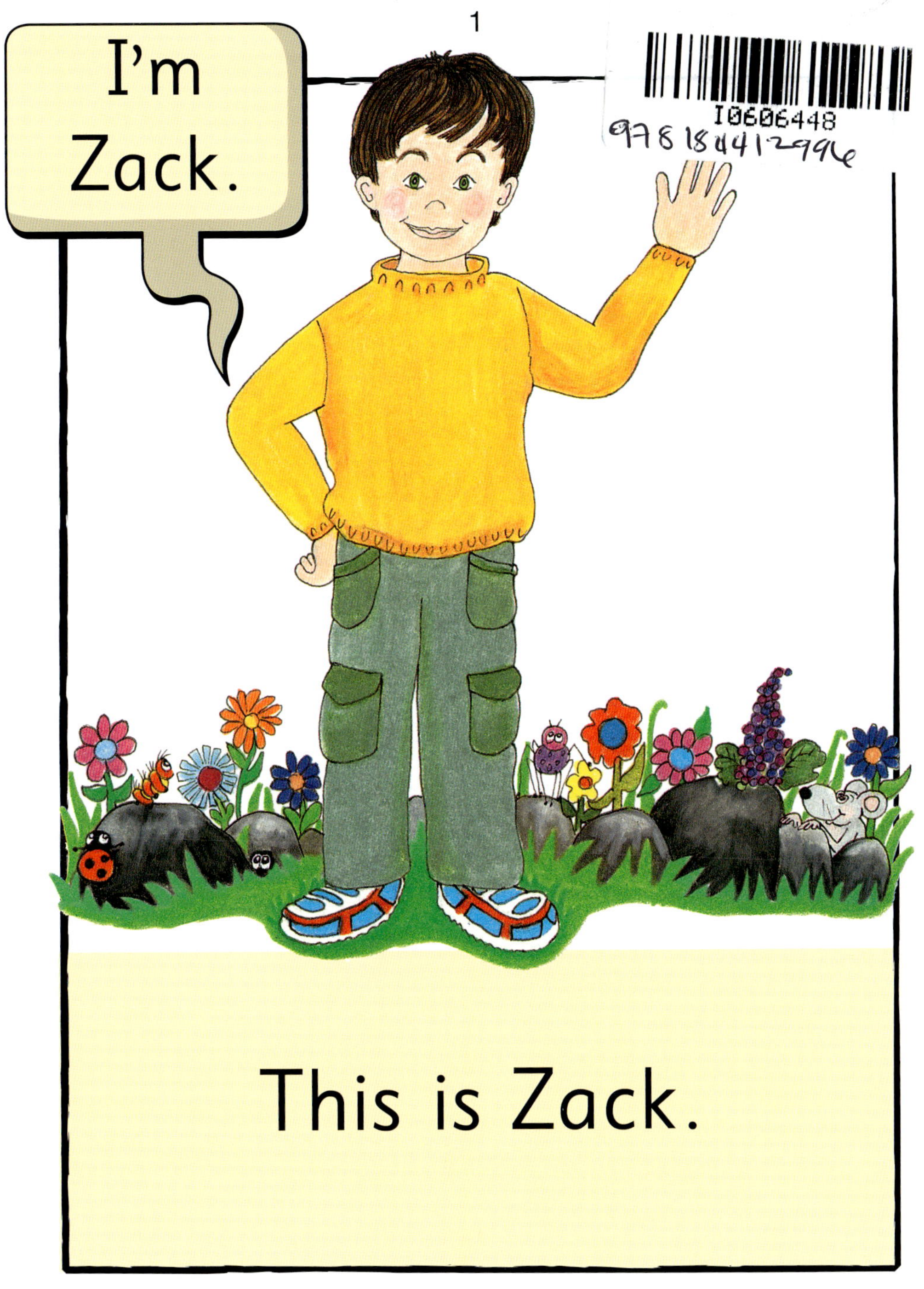

This is Zack.

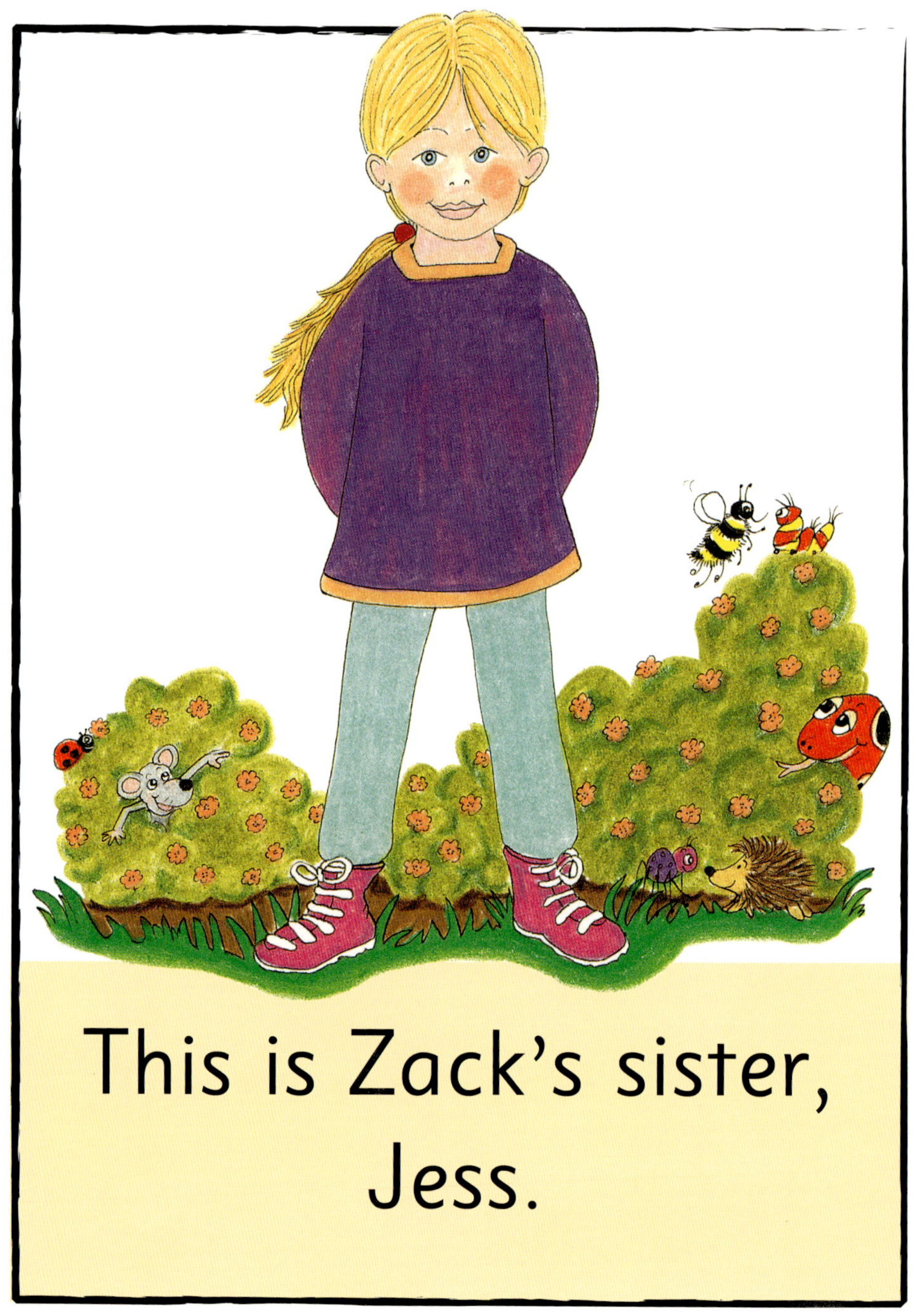

This is Zack's sister, Jess.

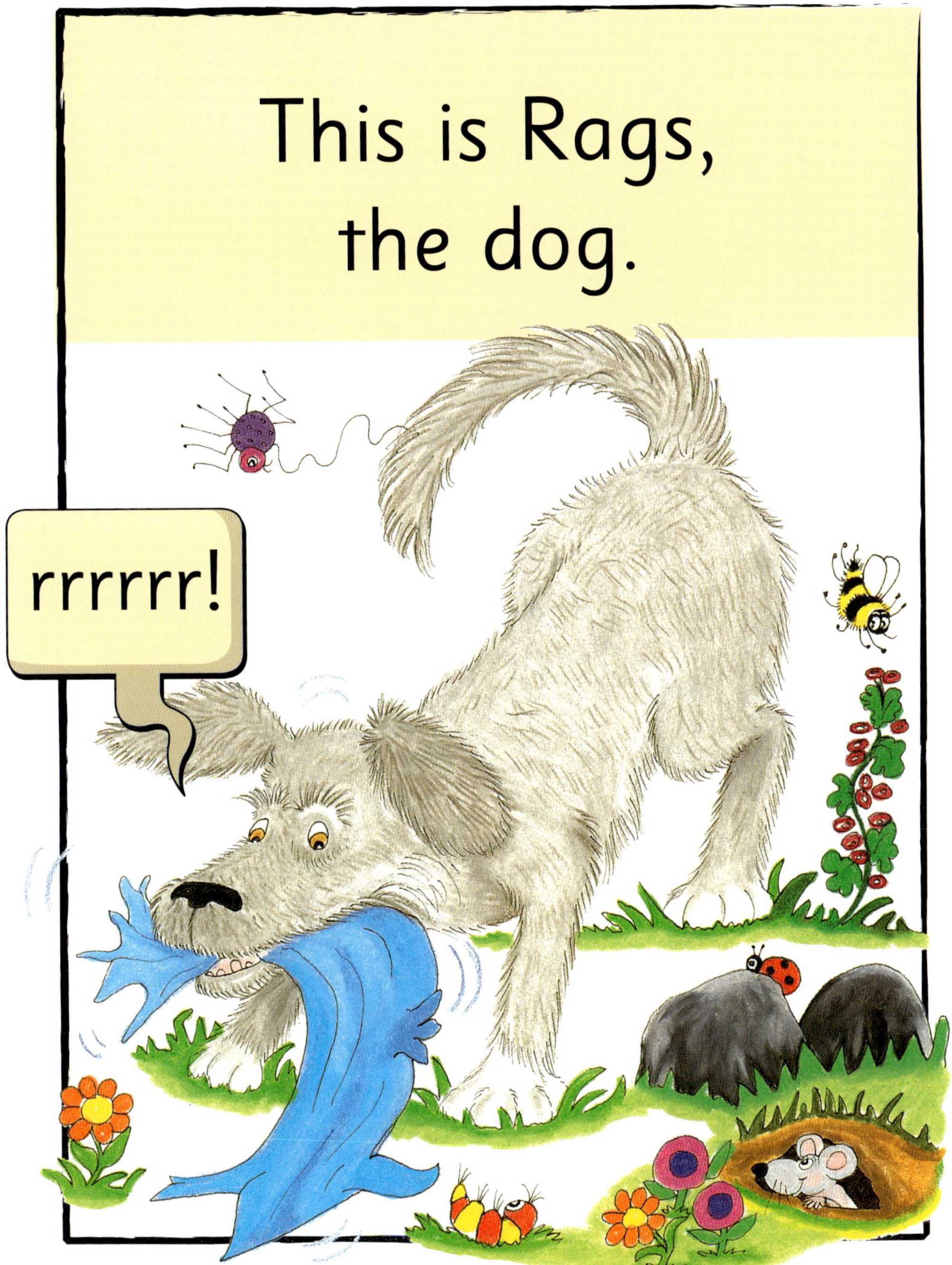
This is Rags,
the dog.
rrrrrr!

Rags, Zack, and Jess are in the garden.

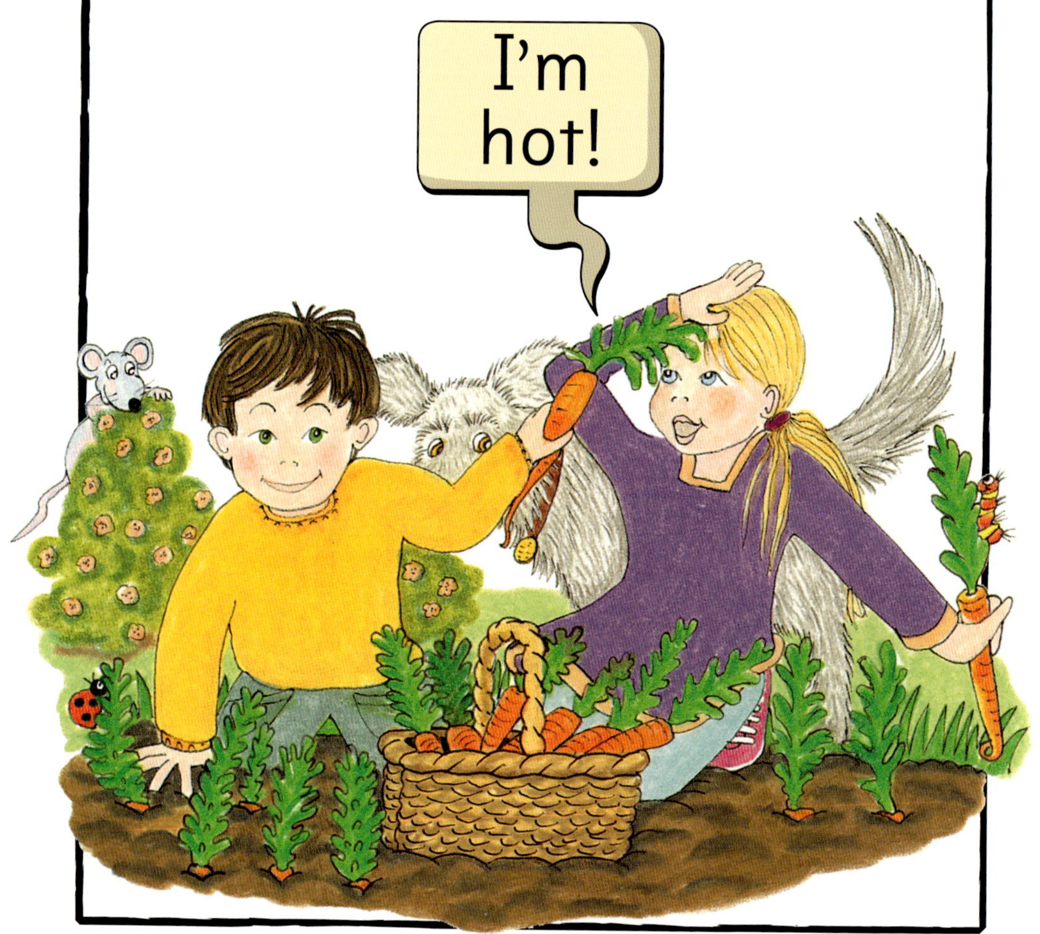

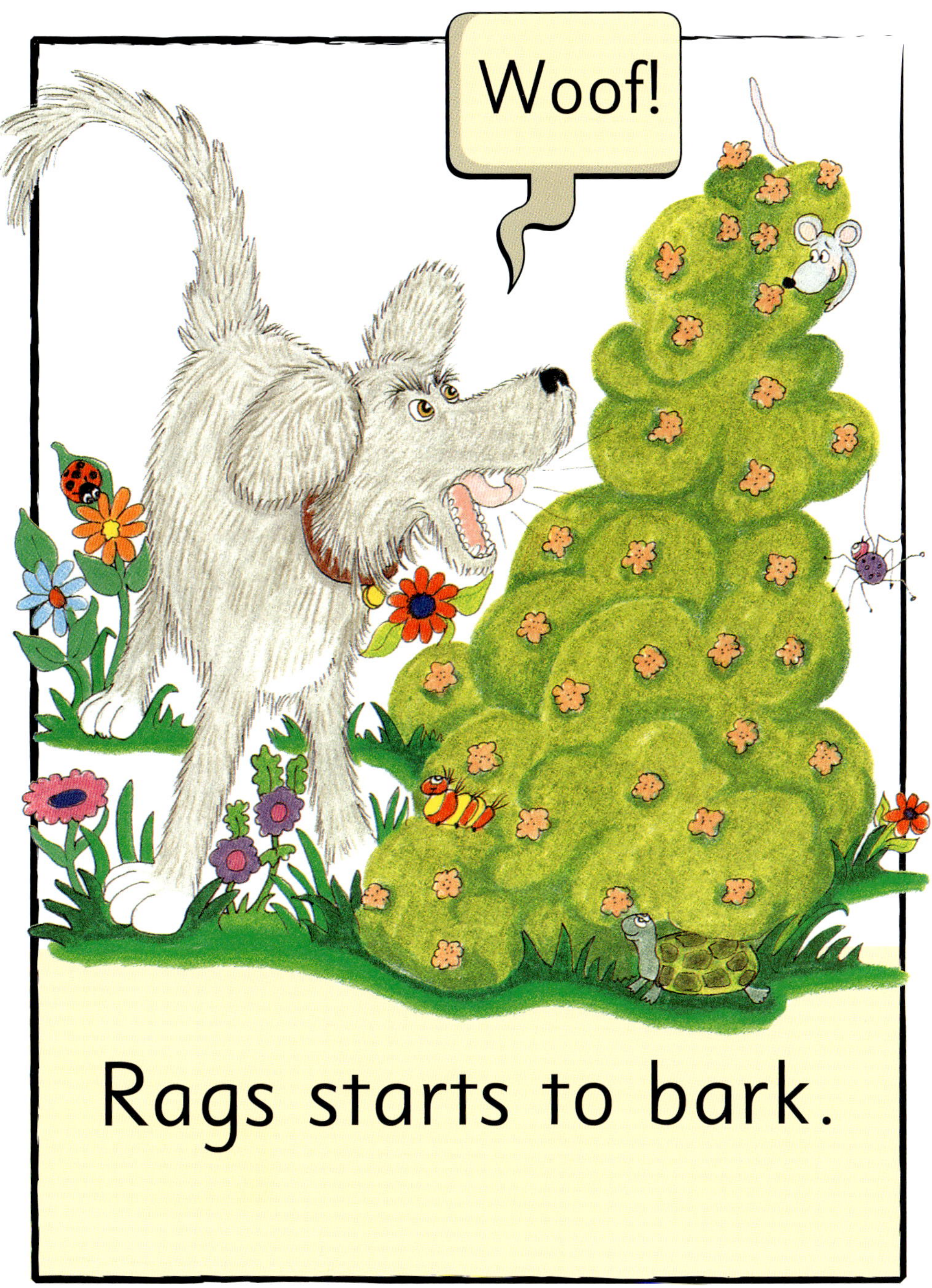

Rags starts to bark.

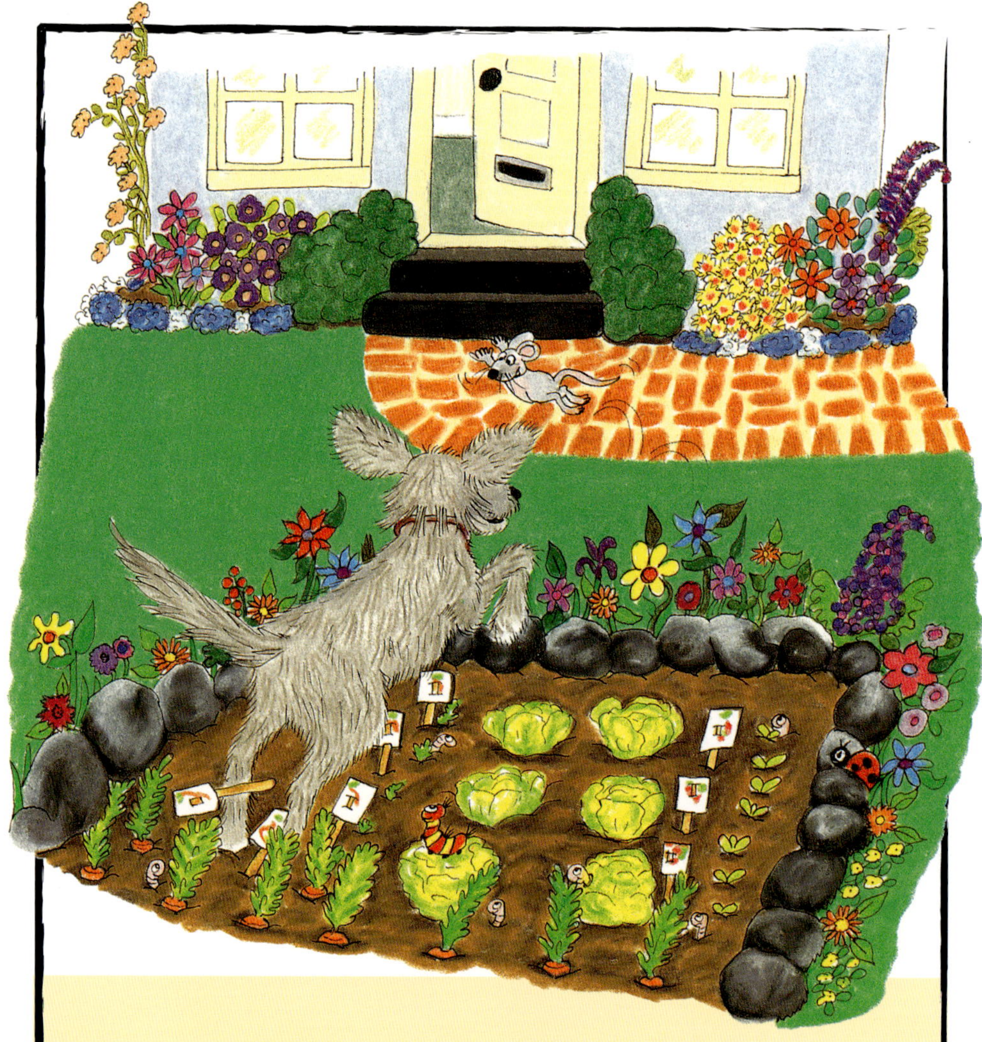

He runs up the garden to the house.

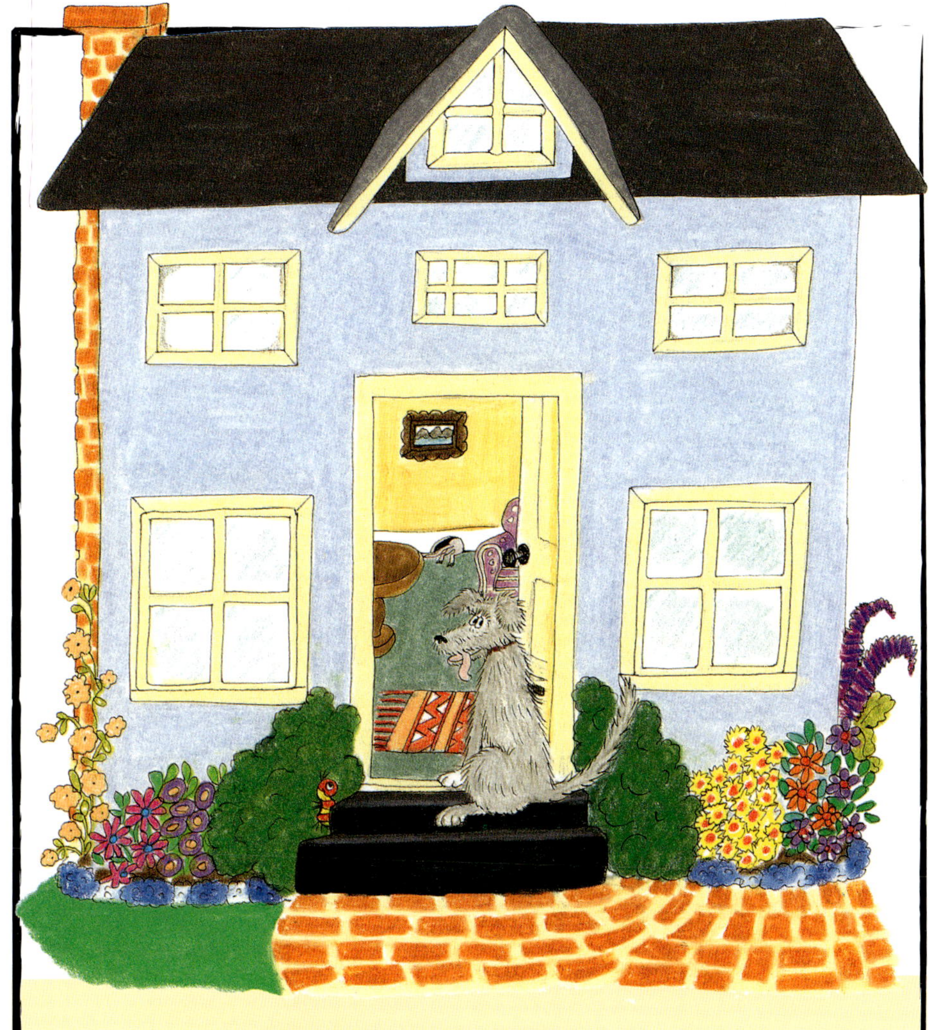

This is Zack
and Jess's house...

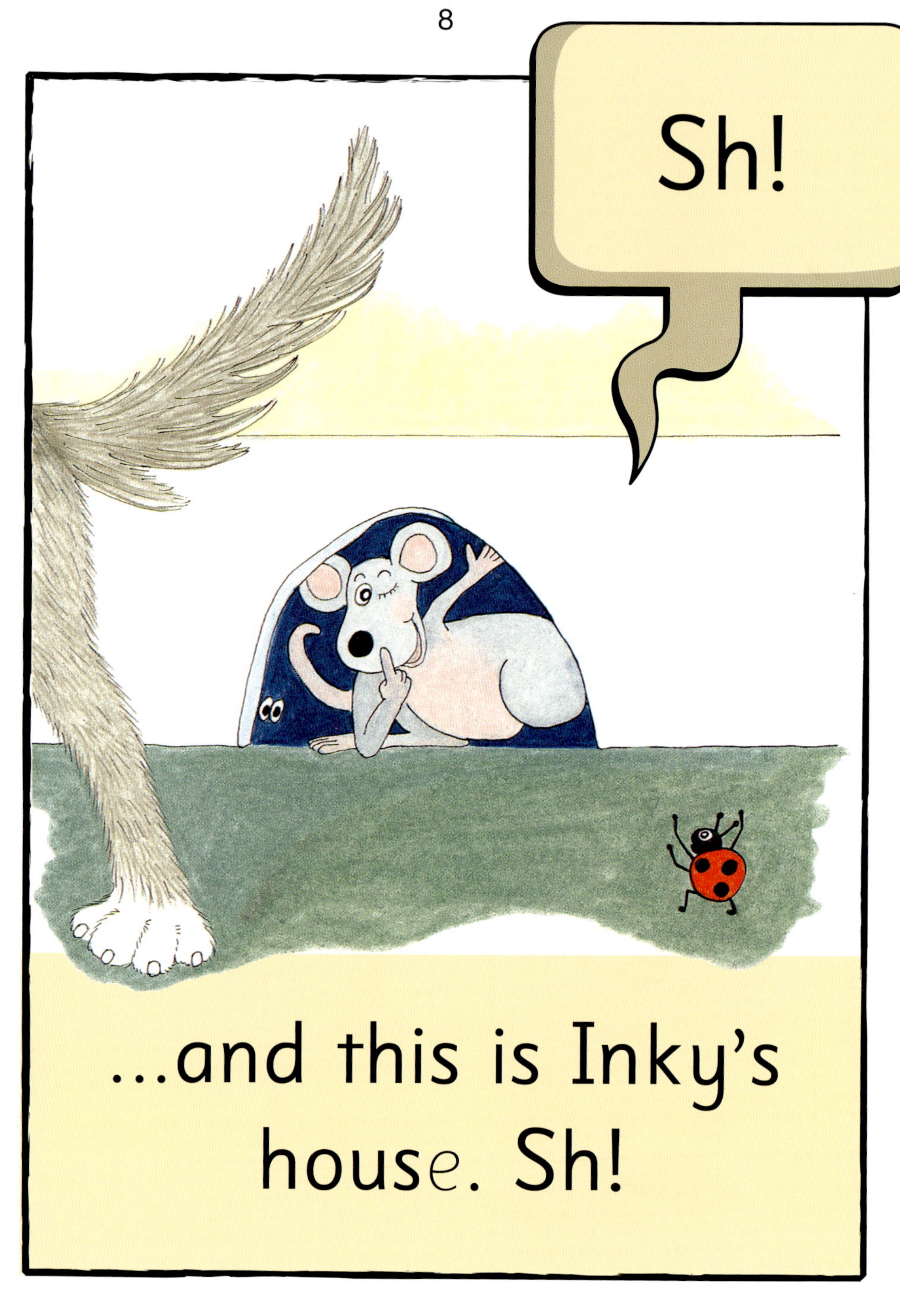

...and this is Inky's house. Sh!